MUTED VOICES

WE PLAN, WE PROMISE, FATE WINS

MUTED VOICES

WE PLAN, WE PROMISE, FATE WINS

TAWSEEF AHMAD BHAT.

PAPER TOWNS
PUBLISHERS

PAPER TOWNS
PUBLISHERS

First published by

Papertowns Publishers
72, Vishwanath Dham Colony,
Niwaru Road, Jhotwara,
Jaipur, 302012

Muted Voices

ISBN Print Book – 978-93-6185-549-8

Printed in India

DEDICATION

When I think about this dedication part. Two thoughts visit me. One is what made me write this book and the second is what made me keep going. A part of this first thought carries my old self who is still within me, dead or abandoned. Trying to search itself or maybe running away. The another part of this thought is "Her". Her, who had her own name when she set foot in my life and I welcomed her with another name which took me 2 days to make. So I gave her this second name "Akhibah". Her stay in my life was never so calm, never so stable, yes it was but very often. She carved her self on the walls of my heart that perhaps I could never erase.

The second thought that visits me belongs to some of my dearest people and some strangers. The dearest people who had always stayed beside or behind me in my every lows. To the family living miles away from me, who make my phone ring everyday or many times a day. To the ones living here with me providing me a feel not less than a family. To those friends who are always there to listen my non-sense talks, who are always there to do their best for the friendship if they can. who don't even laugh for weeks but will surely make me laugh with their typed messages.

And many people who always wished me best and kept there support.

Here are now these strangers who are a part of this dedication. They are the couples I often see on roads holding their hands.The old man working by road side for a family which is living miles away from him. The people who see my art and raise their hands and their voice saying “keep it up”.

PREFACE

Some voices are not silenced by force.

They are muted by time, by habit, by the quiet agreement to endure.

This book is made of those voices.

Not the ones that shout or demand attention. But the thoughts that arrive late at night and and stuck within our hearts. The sentences you rehearse in your head and never say out loud. The truths you lower your volume for, because the world prefers comfort over accuracy.

Each page stands alone because that is how these voices exist—in fragments, interruptions, brief moments of honesty before life resumes its noise. There is no order to follow here. No lesson plan. No promise of resolution.

Some pages may feel unfinished. That is not a flaw. That is the point. Most inner truths never reach completion; they only surface, whisper, and retreat.

This book does not aim to explain you to yourself.It simply refuses to let certain thoughts die unheard.

Read it if you ever found your own voices stuck in you.

Read it if you ever felt unheard.

Read it if you have a silent soul. . .

ABOUT BOOK

Muted voices is a collection of brief writings which hold the things we swallow, thoughts buried to keep the peace.Each piece is brief, almost quiet. This is not fiction, not a decorative poetry, not comfort writing.It is a record of self-silencing and voices muted by love,fear, duty,and survival.Read it slowly. Or don't read it at all. But if you have ever learned to stay quiet to remain intact,this book is for you.

ABOUT AUTHOR

I belong to a profession, i never chose but now i love it. Same happened with this writing part of my life. I didn't chose it. From just journaling to being an aspiring writer.From writing usually to loving it and finding it a means of shelter and getting passionate towards it. My own words often raise doubts against my identity though i am seeking my identity within these words.My writing has been an alteration of inner grief into acceptance. I am none but one who is somehow alienated.

PROLOGUE

There has always been a moment in my life where I find myself seeking the meaning of everything; straights and turns ,ups and bumps ,downs and drowns but never I found a true meaning of anything .It is perhaps because I hadn't gone to the peak of that moment or situation, like; yes I have been lonely but maybe loneliness was farther ,yes I failed but may be failure was farther ,yes I was abandoned by the ones whom I loved but maybe I didn't got that peak abandonment. same was with love, I always wished to have a dream love story of mine, which I sought here and there, which I assumed; is the one I was within. and maybe was the one which is still stuck or which I had been in when it was my last togetherness with love. Which has no existence presently but exists as an illusion in my soul. All this I faced, I tried to seek the meaning behind it. What I found and what I remained from is what you are going to read ahead.

Go through these silent voices that are now
in the shape of words.
The voices that were never heard
perhaps were ignored
or the listening ears failed.
I hope the eyes won't fail.
I hope my words won't fail.

Sometimes I think

Love doesn't exist

It is an illusion.

Then I see my heart calming down

On even those late replies of you.

I wish if you had loved me in October.

The same way you loved me in February.

I might never bring you

The moon and the stars

But I would surely serve you

Poems on dinner.

There are hearts

That keep enduring

Because consistent endurance

makes them embrace it.

They had given a

wrong definition of love.

Love is a blessing for those

who are loved and

curse for lovers.

There is a poem stuck in my throat

Feeling like a rope around my neck

Tightening every night

Shortening my breath

Making me feel death.

Some people don't die

The natural or accidental

Death. Though they are killed

By this undiscovered parasite

Which invades their soul.

After being miles away

I had to visit you,

I had to see you, hold your hand

Fingers intervined,whispering you “I love you”

But how sad that I can now only visit you in my dreams

So do I, oh! Beautiful you..

Whenever you asked me to speak

It was me who stayed mute,

My heart always screamed your name.

I was done with my life

When you made your entry

Now I am tired of promises

But I would never be tired of loving you.

There have been moments

Me watching your photo

And

Tears making their ways

over my face.

When you feel too cold

Like frozen, remember

It is that part of night

Closer to sunrise.

I was brave enough to extinguish

This fire inside me!

Wait, no

If I was brave, why did I

Chose this pen.

Whenever I open my wallet

And see your photo

I find my heart giggling with my soul.

Loving you is a grief filled mercy

Which I wish to never end

Though you could have stayed and let it be

Just mercybut your separation filled it.

What if I died in winter

Where from will they

Bring the flowers.

While searching for peace

I found pieces which

belonged to my heart.

But no piece I found

Within the person who shattered it.

What would you call a person

Who has never uttered a word

A mute or a writer.

Do what stiches you heart

Not what shatters it

Obviously, you are

Broken.

I wish to receive the flowers now,

which i am going to receive on

my death.

They were teaching the

lessons of love.

I faked a sick leave

How unfortunate

I remained from learning this love.

My father was once a gardener

He had a beautiful Garden

and always called me a blossoming flower

Now I see Myself, my heart, my soul

All turned into deserts.

May be dreams are a

A kind of birds

Which we cage in our childhood

And when turn young

We free them up.

If I am given a choice between

me and my old self, I am afraid

I might choose her.

How ironic that I am

intensely introverted

But still, I talk a lot

But to myself.

Realised a fact that

We all are selfish.

Every single act or step we take

Is for our own self

Often in love

We apprise everything we do

While knowing

We did it all

For the happiness

Of our own..

If it was a pen

I would have inked it down

If it was a paper

I would have filled it

With words

If it was a place

I would have

Abandoned it.

If it was a word

I would have turned mute

Though I am

But unfortunately, it was my heart.

How could I say

It is your fault.

Surely, the fault was mine.

I couldn't understand you

Though I couldn't

Understand myself.

It is our body that dies once

But our hearts die again and

Again, maybe every day.

There is no person

Who could understand

Your heart, you are the one

Supposed to heal,

Supposed to get ready to die again,

They were just

Medical professionals

And still they added "cage"

Word to the ribs

Rest you know why.

For so many years

Iam running

Still there is this

Street sign board

“You have miles to go”.

Give me a country I will

Take care of it

But don't give me a heart

The pieces of mine will pierce it.

If given a night to stay

In a noisy city or

Silent woods, I would choose

The city though it chose me

However, the night knows

Where do I belong.

Still now, I would have

Bursted myself in this rain

Like I always did in my past.

But, sadly, now I have a

Meeting to attend

A workplace to reach

A shift to do

A boss to listen.

There is a suffering

You pay your young age for it

The so-called childhood trauma.

How would I accept I am

A human being though

I never treated myself like one.

Childhood gave me trauma

My younger self gave me

Heartbreak

I wonder, what tragedy

This adulthood will bring.

I wonder about the people

Behind bars, they are

Actually free.

When my dad used to scold me

I used to go to my mother

Now where shall I go

When my boss scolds me.

I always dreamt of flying like a bird

Now realised

Not all birds are supposed to fly.

It was until I locked my gaze at my shadow
At the sunset time, I realised how the
Separations occur, no matter what.

I was promised a palm tree and was offered

A cactus. how would I say

People are sweet.

You offered me shelter when

I didn't even need.

And snatched my boots

When I had to run.

You say you love me

But the messages still

Didn't turned blue.

when in love, don't promise.

you may die

even before fulfilling the promises

or

you may leave.

In the midst of nights, you will call, you will cry
Knowing no ears are hearing. But still, you will call
until your own heart cries through the tears of eyes
and you will find, you are the only listener, to yourself.

How ironic that

besides knowing that I am a mute

You made me sing.

You wanted the world hear and listen me.

But you yourself remained from listening

Me, my silences.

Give me a moment of peace

I will offer you any piece of my heart.

So, you get to know how desperate I am

for even a moment of peace,

a moment of you.

You often taunted me of my silences

Though I was mute, but a listener to you

One could never have.

Sunset moments, bursting in rain,
Such moments faded when you came
After you left, I wished them back
They never came. loneliness stayed.

The moment I go to bed

I feel like I entered a desert

Darkness of room

Like the sand storm

I scream silently

I yearn breaths

I die.

I often get jealous of my own heart

It has eyes and the tears

It speaks out

I am mute, I stay silent

To whom shall I speak

How could I speak.

On The journey of love

I didn't found any footprints

Of our love, what I found was

A path of regrets.

If you faced loneliness, failure

Confusion, anxiety

And failed love

You are a loser

Who will never lose.

Where shall one go

When abandoned from his favourite places

Evicted from the heart he loved and

Not destined anymore.

I would have given up these breaths

And eventually the beats of heart

But

They often reminded me of you.

We will meet someday

I might not speak a word

I might see you and forget to

Turn my eyes off you.

I might faint

I might die

I wish you be gentle for once then.

I would have told you

"I don't love you anymore

But whenever I try to,

I forget, I forget myself

I forget everything.

How cruel am i

God blessed me with a tongue,

A clear throat,

A bunch of languages,

Perhaps people who could have listened

But I

I didn’t utter a word

I behaved like a mute.

I wonder ,what tragedy made me so.

I have been called a best friend

I have been called a best boy

I have been called a best salesman

I have been called a best lover

But I was only proud when

I was called a kindest person.

We people are so ignorant

That we forget the moments

Where we had wished for the moments

We have now in ignorance.

She is beautifull

Her hair is beautiful

Her eyes are beautiful

I might end up writing books

On her beauty.

But the most beautiful thing is

She is true.

When we met

i found her shattered

like the dead autumnal leaf

about to fall.

A withered flower

That was supposed to blossom

Her fragile heart

Her innocent soul.

But She doesn't know

What was I then.

Love has wonders within it

How would then someone

Leave for her/him self

And someone stay while

Forgetting her/himself.

I was loved and I loved

And then while staying in this

Ocean of love,

I realized, the main thing to keep love

In its true form is to respect it.

I am still in that small world of ours

Waiting at the door,

Your promises wandering around

I am afraid of your delayed return

Or no return

This wait has enervated me

I might fall

And never wake to that world again.

I was always concerned over finding love,

I ended up realising the beauty of

the friendships

Which I had found already

How easily we people have

Taken this love.

The love that came creating

Greatest stories since

Adam and eve, along through

Laila majnu, heer ranjha.

Ruining it sometimes for Egos

I came so long in this journey
Of love, I have given your name to a fictional character
who is always around me.

How beautiful it would have been

I watering the flowers in the garden

You watching me from the windows

With half asleep eyes.

I'm afraid,

Some morning I might wake up

without having dreams of you

perhaps I could forget you.

There were a lot of aches

That my heart had suffered

And still it endured the pain of

Our separation.

Its endurance often Terrifies me.

Today your return might heal me

It might mend my heart

But tomorrow it might not affect me.

I wonder about my silences

The concealed emotions within my heart

keep wondering me

How grateful that I can write

So you can read and feel

The MUTED VOICES

Which stayed trapped

Beneath my heart.